W9-BTP-103

Magic
JOHNSON

MAGIC JOHNSON
Basketball Star & Entrepreneur

By J Chris Roselius

ABDO
Publishing Company

Content Consultant: Juan Javier Pescador
Professor of History, Michigan State University

Published by ABDO Publishing Company, 8000 West 78th Street, Edina, Minnesota 55439. Copyright © 2011 by Abdo Consulting Group, Inc. International copyrights reserved in all countries. No part of this book may be reproduced in any form without written permission from the publisher. SportsZone™ is a trademark and logo of ABDO Publishing Company.

Printed in the United States of America,
North Mankato, Minnesota
112010
012011

Editor: Matt Tustison
Copy Editor: Paula Lewis
Series Design: Christa Schneider
Cover Production: Christa Schneider
Interior Production: Christa Schneider

Library of Congress Cataloging-in-Publication Data
Roselius, J Chris.
  Magic Johnson : basketball star and entrepreneur / by J Chris Roselius.
     p. cm. — (Legendary athletes)
  Includes bibliographical references and index.
  ISBN 978-1-61714-756-2
  1. Johnson, Earvin, 1959—-Juvenile literature. 2. Basketball players—United States—Biography—Juvenile literature. 3. African American basketball players—Biography—Juvenile literature. 4. Businessmen—United States—Biography—Juvenile literature. 5. African American businesspeople—Biography—Juvenile literature. I. Title.
  GV884.J63R67 2011
  796.323092—dc22
  [B]
                            2010046696

TABLE OF
CONTENTS

The Lakers' Magic Johnson, *right*, and Kareem Abdul-Jabbar double-team the 76ers' Caldwell Jones in the 1980 NBA Finals. Johnson, a rookie, helped Los Angeles win the title in six games.

A Legend Is Born

On May 16, 1980, the National Basketball Association (NBA) and its fans witnessed an NBA Finals performance that is still regarded as one of the best ever. The Los Angeles Lakers were in Philadelphia to face the 76ers in Game 6. As the teams prepared for the game, the Lakers' Earvin "Magic" Johnson entered the circle at midcourt for the opening tip.

Typically, the center on each team participates in the jump ball to start a basketball game. The Lakers' center, Kareem Abdul-Jabbar, was the star of his team and one of the best players in the NBA. During the regular season, Abdul-Jabbar had led the Lakers in scoring, rebounding, and blocked shots. He was selected as the league's Most Valuable Player (MVP) for a record sixth time.

But in Game 5 of the Finals in Los Angeles, Abdul-Jabbar suffered a badly sprained left ankle. The injury would force him to sit out Game 6. Needing someone to fill in for Abdul-Jabbar, interim coach Paul Westhead decided to go with Johnson, the 20-year-old rookie, at center when the Lakers were on offense and put him back at guard when the team was on defense.

Johnson was a one-of-a-kind player. He was 6 feet, 9 inches (2.06 m) tall and weighed 215 pounds (97.52 kg). Players his size usually are forwards in the NBA and do not dribble the ball very often. But Johnson was a point guard. He dribbled the ball up the court and

A Different NBA

The 1980 NBA Finals featured a fantastic matchup between Los Angeles and Philadelphia, but many people never watched the games, mostly because they were not regularly televised live around the country. In 1980, the Finals started on May 4 and ran through May 16. Unlike today, the league was not very popular and did not have many viewers.

Despite its television deal with the NBA, Columbia Broadcasting System (CBS) did not want to interrupt its prime-time television schedule during May with basketball. The solution CBS came up with was to have weekday games air after the local news, meaning the games would not be shown until 11:30 p.m. in Philadelphia. Even on the West Coast, the games were shown on tape delay after the news, except in Los Angeles, where the games were broadcast live.

After watching the show Magic Johnson put on in the Finals, the NBA soon made changes. Once its contract with CBS expired after the 1980–81 season, the NBA demanded that all Finals games be shown during prime time. The league also pushed back the start of the season from October to November, allowing the Finals to be played, and aired, in June instead of May. The TV networks do not show as many new episodes of their shows in June, which meant the Finals would have less competition for viewers.

ran the offense for the Lakers. Johnson's outstanding rookie season quieted critics who said he would be too big and slow to be a successful point guard in the NBA. Now he was a major reason why the Lakers were playing for the title. Even so, asking him to fill in for Abdul-Jabbar was a huge task.

But Johnson did not show any nerves before the game. He was laughing and grinning. Philadelphia's center, Caldwell Jones, was 7-foot-1 (2.16 m) and stood opposite Johnson. Jones looked amazed, not quite sure what to think of Johnson. Jones easily won the jump ball against Johnson, but that would be about the only play Johnson failed to do well that spring night. Dribbling skillfully, Johnson drove past Jones for easy layups. When the 76ers tried to slow him down by having guards defend Johnson, his height allowed him to sink easy jumpers or make uncontested passes to his teammates.

When the contest was over, Johnson had finished one of the greatest games in NBA Finals history. Playing 47 of the game's 48 minutes, he scored 42 points, grabbed 15 rebounds, handed out seven assists, and had three steals and one blocked shot. With Johnson dominating the game, the Lakers, without superstar Abdul-Jabbar, defeated the Sixers 123–107 to win the best-of-seven series and earn their first NBA title since 1972.

"Nobody had expected us to win that game," Johnson wrote in his autobiography *My Life*. "We knew we could do it, and we were up for the game. But to actually have it happen without the greatest player in the league—that was hard to believe."[1]

Continued Success

Johnson's brilliance in Game 6 allowed him to become the first rookie in league history to be named the MVP of the NBA Finals. Fans, however, should not have been too surprised by what he did on the court against the 76ers. After leading Michigan State to victory in the 1979 National Collegiate Athletic Association (NCAA) title game—in which the Spartans beat future Hall of Fame player Larry Bird and Indiana State—Johnson was the first player selected in the NBA Draft. Despite his young age, Johnson proved that he belonged in the NBA. Johnson was selected to the All-Star Game as a rookie and finished the season averaging 18 points, 7.7 rebounds, and 7.3 assists.

Johnson was even better in the playoffs, averaging 18.3 points, 10.5 rebounds, and 9.4 assists per game. He almost averaged a triple-double in his first NBA postseason. His performance in the Finals, specifically Game 6, left no doubt as to his skill.

"I knew he was good, but I never realized he was great,"[2] Doug Collins, a 76ers guard, said.

Lakers star rookie Magic Johnson holds his NBA Finals MVP Award as he poses with interim coach Paul Westhead in May 1980.

Just a Big Kid

When Johnson first arrived in Los Angeles and started practicing with the older players, they quickly noticed his incredible energy and enthusiasm. Johnson was quick to give a high five to a teammate for making a good play. Johnson's child-like approach to playing basketball brought energy to the team.

Lakers coach Jack McKinney, who was unable to finish the season on the bench after suffering a serious

King of the Triple-Double

During Magic Johnson's rookie season, he often reached double figures in scoring, rebounding, and assists. He would accomplish the feat so often, the term "triple-double" was created to describe his statistical accomplishment. By the end of his career, Johnson had 138 triple-doubles, ranking second in NBA history. Only Oscar Robertson, with 181 career triple-doubles, had exceeded Johnson as of 2010.

head injury in a bicycle accident during the season, said Johnson changed the style of basketball the Lakers played, making it more exciting. In previous seasons, Los Angeles slowed the pace of the game down and fed the ball in the paint—the area near the basket—to Abdul-Jabbar, Adrian Dantley, and its other big players. In a word, the Lakers were "bland"—until Johnson arrived.

Johnson's seemingly unlimited potential was fully on display against Philadelphia, and his one-man demolition of the 76ers in Game 6 left a lasting impression on Philadelphia star Julius "Dr. J." Erving.

"Earvin turned in what many consider, myself included, the best performance ever in an NBA Finals game," Erving said. "While I obviously would've preferred winning that game and then the championship, at least I can look back 25 years later and say that I saw the legend of Magic Johnson born first-hand."[3]

Lakers coach Jack McKinney is shown with Magic Johnson a month before the 1979–80 season opened.

CHAPTER 2

Early in his NBA career, Magic Johnson poses for a picture with his father, Earvin Sr. Magic learned from his father's strong work ethic.

Growing Up

Earvin Johnson Jr. was born in Lansing, Michigan, on August 14, 1959, to Christine and Earvin Johnson Sr. With the birth of Earvin Jr., the Johnson family had seven children. Earvin Sr. had three children from a previous marriage. He and Christine would have three more children after Earvin Jr. was born.

The family was not rich, but Earvin's parents worked hard to provide for the children. Earvin Sr. worked at a nearby General Motors factory and held down two part-time jobs. This allowed the Johnsons to live in a three-bedroom house. One room was shared by Earvin's four sisters—Pearl, Kim, and twins Evelyn and Yvonne. Earvin slept in the same room as his two older brothers—Quincy and Larry. Earvin's stepbrother and stepsisters— Michael, Lois and Mary—often came to visit as well, meaning Earvin usually had a playmate nearby.

As an adult, Johnson has been known for his smile and playful personality. Those traits must have carried over from childhood—Earvin's mother often described him as a playful baby who loved to smile and be held by anyone. Before he became known as Magic, Earvin had many different nicknames. His parents called him Junior, and his friends called him E. J. or E. Neighbors often called him June Bug because he was chubby as a child and always hopping around.

"I'm glad I didn't have to go through my professional career with *that* name," Johnson wrote. "'And now, ladies and gentlemen, playing guard for the world-champion Los Angeles Lakers, June Bug Johnson!'"[1]

The Value of Hard Work

Earvin looked up to his father and saw how hard he worked. Earvin learned that he was expected to work hard as well. He had to do his share of chores, including raking leaves or shoveling snow. Earvin also had to work for spending money as his father did not believe in handing out money without someone earning it. By the age of ten, Earvin started his own yard-care business. This enabled Earvin to see a movie or buy a record.

Earvin also helped clean the offices of two prominent African-American businessmen in Lansing. For the most part, Lansing was a white community. There were not very many rich African-American men.

But these two men had large homes and expensive cars. Earvin was determined that he would become successful like these men.

Basketball in the Genes

Earvin's father rarely had free time, but when he did have a chance to relax, he often watched NBA games on television. Earvin Sr. had played basketball in high school, and Christine had also played basketball when she was young. As Earvin's older brothers played basketball, it was not surprising that Earvin developed an interest in the sport. He also decided that being part of a winning team, not necessarily being a great player, was what mattered most when it came to sports.

Earvin was often seen dribbling a basketball or playing at the local basketball courts. When he was not playing, he listened to his father talk about the game— about details that could help an average player become a good player and a good player become great. Johnson said his father helped him understand the importance of the little things in basketball.

One of the little things meant becoming an excellent ball handler with the ability to dribble and pass the ball well. Earvin dribbled the ball in front of his house for hours. First, he used his right hand, then his left, and then back and forth between both hands. No matter where he went, a basketball was often with him, bouncing up and down off a sidewalk, street, or floor.

The little things also meant practicing the basic shots of basketball. Instead of taking nothing but jump shots away from the basket, Earvin spent much of his time on the playground practicing layups. Positioned close to the basket, he would shoot off the backboard and into the net. Earvin practiced until he became proficient at shooting with either hand, a skill very few people had at his age.

Putting His Skills to Use

By the time Earvin was eight years old, he was better at basketball than the children his own age, so he played against Larry, his older brother. Larry was not only older, but he was also bigger and stronger, giving him the advantage when he got close to the basket and shot. But Earvin did not let that stop him. His practice dribbling the ball and making layups paid off. He would dribble around Larry and make bucket after bucket.

"Watching those NBA games with my father, I studied the great players and tried to learn from them all. Bill Russell was always a favorite of the grown-ups, because they appreciated his brilliant defensive moves. Well, Russell was a great player, all right, but what I admired most about him had nothing to do with his moves. It was all those championships he had won with the Celtics. That's all I ever wanted— to be a winner."[2]

—Magic Johnson, on his favorite NBA player as a child, the Celtics' Bill Russell

As Earvin developed his skills, he also started to grow. His June Bug nickname no longer was appropriate. In seventh grade, he was 6 feet (1.83 m) tall. By the time he was in eighth grade, he was 6-foot-4 (1.93 m). On the basketball court for Dwight Rich Junior High, Earvin was having a great time. He was easily the best player on the team.

Unfortunately for Earvin, his father was always working when the games were played. Earvin did his best to tell his father about each game afterward, but it was not quite the same. Finally, Earvin Sr. asked his supervisor if he could leave work early to go watch his son play. After being turned down, he went straight to the foreman, who said he had heard about Earvin Jr.'s success on the court and that Earvin Sr. had to be there to watch. Earvin Sr. left work early, and, after watching his son, he did not miss another game.

Earvin led his junior high team to two Lansing city championships. Still, he had doubts about his playing abilities. Perhaps he was so good because he was taller than everyone else. Plus, Lansing is just a small city located about 80 miles (128.75 km) northwest of Detroit. The stars of the NBA always seemed to come from Chicago, New York, Los Angeles, or some other large city. Because he was not sure about his talent, Earvin continued to work at improving his skills.

When Magic Johnson was a child, youngsters across the nation were bused in an effort to integrate the schools.

On to High School

In the fall of 1974, Earvin enrolled at Everett High School. Earvin actually lived closer to Sexton High School, a predominately black school. However, because of integration policies during the 1970s, Earvin was bused to Everett. Earvin was not very pleased about being placed in this predominately white school with a mediocre basketball team. Yet, Earvin tried out for the basketball team and earned a place on the varsity team.

However, it was obvious that most of his teammates did not want him there. Despite being wide open during a practice, passes were seldom thrown his way. Deciding he had enough, Earvin took over. He dribbled the ball the length of the court and then slammed the ball through the basket. Again and again, he did everything on his own. This nearly led to a fight between Earvin and one of his teammates. At this point, Earvin considered leaving the team. But after talking to his coach, George Fox, he decided to stay. Soon, he reached an agreement with his teammates, and Everett started to play well.

Even though Earvin was the tallest player on the team, Fox had Earvin play point guard because of his ability to dribble and pass the ball. Earvin made sure his teammates got the ball in the area they wanted it. Thanks to his leadership, Everett turned into a winning team. Earvin played so well during his junior season that he was selected as Michigan's Prep Player of the Year by United Press International and was named MVP of his conference.

As Earvin entered his senior season, Everett was one of the top teams in the state. Earvin had two goals as a senior: He wanted to win a state title and earn a scholarship to play basketball in college. His first goal was reached when Everett captured the title with a thrilling overtime win in the championship game on the University of Michigan campus in Ann Arbor. His second goal was more difficult because multiple schools wanted Earvin to play for them. He narrowed his choices to two schools—the University of Michigan and Michigan State University, in nearby East Lansing.

Friends and fans wanted him to play for Michigan State. Earvin's father wanted him to attend that university. It was the school he had always cheered for, and it was also the school Earvin cheered for when he was younger. Earvin made the decision to attend Michigan State. Soon, he would help change the game of college basketball.

The Birth of Magic

During his sophomore season at Everett High School, Earvin Johnson was already the best player on the team. Playing point guard, he set up his teammates for easy baskets thanks to his amazing passing skills. But Earvin could also score and rebound. In one game, he had 36 points, 18 rebounds, and 16 assists. After the contest, Fred Stabley Jr., a reporter from the *Lansing State Journal*, approached Earvin.

"Listen, Earvin, I think you should have a nickname," Stabley said. "I was thinking of calling you Dr. J., but that's taken. And so is Big E—Elvin Hayes. How about if I call you Magic?"[3]

Earvin was just 15 at the time and embarrassed by the conversation, especially since his teammates were listening. Not thinking the nickname would stick, Earvin said it was fine with him if Stabley wanted to call him Magic. Stabley did not use the nickname right away. But after another impressive game by Earvin, Stabley referred to Earvin "Magic" Johnson in a story. Within months, Earvin became known as Magic throughout Michigan.

In February 1997, former NBA great Magic Johnson received a plaque as Everett High School renamed its gymnasium in honor of him.

CHAPTER 3

Michigan State's Magic Johnson throws a no-look pass as Audie Matthews of Illinois defends in February 1978.

Michigan State Welcomes the Magic Show

When Magic Johnson arrived at Michigan State, the school's basketball team was average at best. The previous season, the Spartans finished 12–15 overall and fifth in the Big Ten Conference with a 9–9 record. But the 1977–78 season would prove to be very different for Michigan State.

Teaming with fellow top recruit Jay Vincent, Johnson led the Spartans to their best season in 11 years. Michigan State reeled off 13 straight wins at one point in the season and captured the school's first Big Ten title since 1967. More importantly, the Spartans advanced to the NCAA tournament, which had only 32 teams during that era, for the first time in 19 years. With Johnson leading the way, the Spartans reached the Mideast Regional title game, which they lost 52–49 to Kentucky. Michigan State ended the year with a 25–5 record.

Teammate Greg Kelser said, "When [Johnson] came in, it became very obvious, along with Jay Vincent, it was obvious that now we were championship-caliber."[1]

Just Better than the Rest

Johnson was outstanding his first college season, averaging 17 points, 7.9 rebounds, and 7.4 assists per game. Those numbers were good enough for him to be named the Big Ten Freshman of the Year. Other players might have scored more points, grabbed more rebounds, or handed out more assists. But there were not many players as well rounded as Johnson. He was a unanimous All-Big Ten selection and the only freshman named to a major All-America team.

Jud Heathcote, coach of Michigan State, said Johnson was not just one of the best players in college basketball, but in the entire country, including the professional ranks. What made Johnson so special, according to Heathcote, was his ability to run the game from the point guard position to make sure his team won. Personal statistics were not as important as victories. Heathcote said,

> In Earvin's case you don't talk about the points he scores, but the points he produces. Not just the baskets and the assists, but the first pass that makes the second pass possible. He's conscious of scoring himself, but it isn't an obsession with him. He doesn't worry about getting his average every game.[2]

Road to the Title

As the 1978–79 season began, two players dominated the college landscape. One was Johnson, thanks to his outgoing personality and ability to make amazing alley-oop passes (passes that led directly to slam dunks) and other spectacular plays. The other was Larry Bird of Indiana State. Just like Johnson, Bird had turned Indiana State into a winning team by his ability to shoot and pass the ball.

Bird's personality, however, was the opposite of Johnson's. Bird rarely spoke to the media, preferring instead to just concentrate on basketball, and he rarely showed any emotion on the court. While Johnson played for Michigan State, a mighty Big Ten school, Indiana State was a small school that played in the Missouri Valley Conference. Some talented players surrounded Johnson. They included Vincent and Kelser, who became the fourth pick in the 1979 NBA Draft by the Detroit Pistons. Bird, meanwhile, was basically a one-man show.

With Bird and Johnson leading their respective teams, Indiana State's Sycamores and Michigan State's

On the *SI* Cover

Before the start of the 1978–79 college season, Magic Johnson was on the cover of the November 27, 1978, *Sports Illustrated* magazine. The image captured Johnson wearing a tuxedo while shooting a layup with the caption, "Michigan State's Classy Earvin Johnson." Johnson has said it is one of his favorite cover shots.

Spartans strung together win after win. Michigan State had a slightly difficult period in conference play, going 4–4 during an eight-game stretch, but when Heathcote allowed the players more freedom on the court, the Spartans took off and claimed another Big Ten title. Meanwhile, Indiana State did not lose during the regular season.

When the NCAA postseason tournament started, Indiana State was the top-ranked team in the country and earned the top seed in the Midwest bracket. Michigan State was the second-seeded team in the Mideast bracket behind the University of Notre Dame. Without a doubt, Johnson and Bird were the two best players in college. The fans wanted to see Michigan State and Indiana State in the title game.

They got their wish. Michigan State rolled through the tournament, beating its opponents by an average of more than 23 points per game in its first four games, including a 101–67 thrashing of the University of Pennsylvania in the national semifinals. Indiana State, meanwhile, struggled after its two opening wins. The Sycamores edged out Arkansas 73–71 in the regional finals and then escaped against DePaul, winning 76–74 in the national semifinals.

But the stage was set—Michigan State versus Indiana State, Johnson versus Bird—for the national championship. Fans, many of whom would see one or

Magic Johnson, *left*, and Larry Bird pose in 1979 before their schools, Michigan State and Indiana State, met for the NCAA title.

both stars play for the first time, could hardly wait for the showdown.

Another Title

Johnson was only a sophomore, but, as it turned out, the 1978–79 season would be his final season at Michigan State. He would declare himself eligible for the NBA Draft after the season. As was the case in high school, Johnson would finish his college career in style.

Johnson and Michigan State defeated Bird and Indiana State 75–64 in the most-watched NCAA final ever. Johnson, who was named the tournament's Most Outstanding Player, had another excellent game, scoring 24 points to go along with seven rebounds and five assists. Bird, meanwhile, struggled against a Michigan State defense that double-teamed him whenever possible. He scored 19 points, but he attempted 21 shots, making only seven. Bird also grabbed 13 rebounds. It was not enough, however, as Johnson walked off the court with the title and a memory that would last a lifetime.

Thanks to the media buzz around the contest, the 1979 title game was the most watched at the time. As of 2010, it still had the highest television rating of any college basketball game ever.

The NCAA quickly took advantage of the new college basketball fans. It increased the number of teams in the tournament from 40 in 1979 to 64 by 1985. As of the 2010–11 season, the tournament included 68 teams. Much of the credit for the tournament's popularity can be given to Bird and Johnson, who helped lift college basketball to a new level.

Magic Johnson helps cut down the net after Michigan State beat Indiana State 75–64 in the 1979 NCAA championship game.

CHAPTER 4

The Lakers' Magic Johnson poses with his NBA Finals
MVP Award alongside first-year coach Pat Riley in June 1982.
Johnson also won a new car for being named MVP.

The Beginning of Showtime

All was going well for Magic Johnson. He had won an NCAA championship at Michigan State in 1979 and followed that with an NBA title in May 1980 with the Lakers in his rookie season. But Johnson's perfect world on the basketball court began to change during his second season in the NBA. On November 11, 1980, the Lakers played against the host Atlanta Hawks. During the game, Hawks center Tom Burleson fell across the back of Johnson's knee.

At first, there appeared to be no injury to Johnson. But one week later, Johnson's left knee was in tremendous pain. Johnson had torn cartilage on the inside of the knee. He would miss nearly four months of the season.

At the time of the injury, Johnson was scoring 21.4 points per game, up from his average of 18 as a rookie, and was leading the NBA in steals and assists. The Lakers' record was 15–5. Without Johnson, they lost five of their next eight games. It was clear Johnson made the difference.

Magic Johnson speaks to reporters on November 26, 1980, about his left knee injury. Johnson missed nearly four months of his second NBA season because of the injury.

With Johnson sidelined, the Lakers rallied around center Kareem Abdul-Jabbar to lead them. The team kept winning, but not at the same pace as when Johnson was in the lineup. It became clear that in order for Los Angeles to win the NBA title again, it would need its point guard on the court.

Johnson began practicing with the Lakers in February and started to travel with the team.

Even though he was not playing yet, the fact that he was back around his teammates provided a lift for the Lakers.

The Return

Johnson was finally cleared to play again. His first game was slated for February 27, 1981, against the New Jersey Nets. His return was a huge event in Los Angeles. Johnson admitted he was excited, but he also said he was nervous and a little scared.

Johnson entered the game with little more than five minutes left in the first quarter. The fans gave him a huge ovation, but they also watched his every move, worried that his repaired knee was not completely healed. Johnson moved normally on the court, but that was about all that was normal during the first quarter.

Johnson missed his first two shots and made some bad passes. But he started to get into the flow of the game in the second quarter, making baskets and diving on the floor for a loose ball. It was quickly apparent that Johnson was back. He helped the Lakers defeat the Nets 107–103.

A Surprising Loss

During the rest of the regular season, Johnson was back in form. The Lakers went 11–6 with Johnson in the lineup again and had a five-game winning streak

Playing to the Music

Before playing a game, Magic Johnson always listened to music. Not only did it fire him up, but, according to Johnson, he played basketball to a beat. Sometimes when he was playing a game, a song would pop into his mind to help him maintain that beat.

heading into the final two games of the regular season. Facing the Utah Jazz and then the Denver Nuggets, Los Angeles lost both games in overtime to finish with a 54–28 record.

Losing two straight games heading to the playoffs was not the way the Lakers wanted to finish the regular season. However, they would face the Houston Rockets in the first round of the playoffs. The Rockets had not won half their games, ending the regular season 40–42. The Lakers were expected to sweep the best-of-three series.

But Houston had other plans. With Moses Malone leading the way, the visiting team defeated Los Angeles 111–107 in the first game. The two teams traveled to Houston for Game 2 of the series, and the Lakers pulled out a 111–106 victory. The play returned to Los Angeles for Game 3. But that did not matter as the Rockets stunned Johnson and his teammates by winning 89–86 with Mike Dunleavy sinking a jump shot with 15 seconds remaining to seal the victory. With the loss, the Lakers were eliminated from the playoffs.

Johnson was blamed for the early playoff exit. His return to the lineup in February had forced the team to make abrupt changes. Norm Nixon went from shooting guard to point guard and then back to shooting guard, and Nixon said that switching positions disrupted his game. There were rumors that the players were upset by the attention Johnson received during his comeback from the knee injury, which hurt the team's chemistry. Johnson was not pleased with the reports. But things would get even worse at the start of the 1981–82 season.

New Coach Comes Aboard

During Johnson's first two seasons, the Lakers liked to run the fast break and have a quick tempo on offense. But heading into the 1981–82 season, Paul Westhead, who had become the permanent coach the previous season, decided that he wanted to feature Abdul-Jabbar a little more on offense, and the coach designed more plays that would get the ball to the center first on offense.

The Lakers opened the season with a double-overtime loss to Houston on national television. A loss to the Phoenix Suns dropped the Lakers to 1–3. This was not the kind of start anyone expected. Owner Jerry Buss was not happy either, citing a lack of excitement on offense. "Showtime," the word Buss had used to describe the team's exciting style of play the previous two seasons, was gone.

The Lakers started to turn things around, winning six of their next seven games to improve to 7–4. But Johnson was not happy with the offense. Even though the team won five straight games, Westhead was fired. Assistant coach Pat Riley was named as the new head coach. Riley believed in the up-tempo offense the Lakers had run in the past.

In their first game under Riley, the Lakers ran past the San Antonio Spurs 136–116. Johnson had 20 points, 16 assists, and 10 rebounds. And he had fun.

"Yeah, I'm happy, and so are him and him and him," Johnson said, gesturing toward the empty lockers of teammates Abdul-Jabbar, Nixon, and forward Jamaal Wilkes.[1]

Meanwhile, many said Johnson was the reason Westhead had been fired. The two had met and discussed how Johnson had not been running the offense the way Westhead wanted it to be run. Johnson said he would rather be traded than play in Westhead's offense. The next day, Westhead was fired.

Johnson asked,

Why was it wrong for me to talk? Should I shut up and be unhappy and jeopardize the team, waiting for something to blow up? Ask anyone who saw us. We were the dullest team in the league. I'd look at films and say, "What is this?" We would get dressed before games and there would be no enthusiasm, nothing; we'd all just sit there.[2]

Showtime Returns, and So Does Another Title

With Riley in charge, Showtime was back at the Forum, the Lakers' home arena, and the team was having fun. Los Angeles went 50–21 during the rest of the 1981–82 regular season and rarely scored fewer than 100 points in a game. The Lakers finished 57–25 for the best record in the Western Conference and received a bye, meaning they did not have to play in the first round of the playoffs. In the postseason, the Lakers were nearly perfect. They won four consecutive games against Phoenix to sweep their opening-round

The Bad Guy

When the Lakers fired coach Paul Westhead, many fans assumed he was fired because Magic Johnson no longer liked playing in his offensive system. Johnson knew he was going to be cast as the villain, so he was ready when the Lakers played their first game in the Forum after Pat Riley was hired.

"I know I'm going to be booed, but I have to deal with it," Johnson said before the game. "As long as I know in my heart that I didn't try to get [Westhead] fired, I can handle it."[3]

After being loudly booed during player introductions, Johnson quickly went to work to turn those boos into cheers. After a solid first quarter, Johnson scored 14 points in the second quarter and added four rebounds and five assists.

By the end of the game, the Lakers had scored 136 points, 30 of them coming on fast breaks, more than they had in any game under Westhead that season. The boos quickly disappeared as Johnson was cheered for his play on the court.

series—the Western Conference semifinals. Los Angeles then swept San Antonio in four games in the Western Conference finals to advance to the NBA Finals against the Philadelphia 76ers.

The series was expected to be close, but the Lakers captured the NBA title, their second in three years over Philadelphia, by defeating the 76ers four games to two. Johnson was named Finals MVP for the second time in his three-season career. According to him, the experience the team went through when Westhead was fired turned out to be key in winning the title.

"All that stuff that happened kind of brought us together," Johnson said. The players had started going out together—to discos and movies. "It's funny sometimes, eight giants sitting in a row at the movies," he added.[4]

Two-Year Wait

The next season did not end with a title for the Lakers, but it was not because of a poor performance by Johnson or any discord. Los Angeles finished 58–24 in 1982–83, again giving the team the best record in the Western Conference. But the Lakers were swept in four games by the 76ers in the NBA Finals. Philadelphia was simply too good. The Sixers had added Malone to an already talented roster of players that included Julius "Dr. J." Erving. The next season, Los Angeles

Lakers guard Magic Johnson goes up for a layup during the 1982 NBA Finals against the 76ers. Los Angeles won the series in six games.

finished 54–28 and again advanced to the NBA Finals, this time against the Boston Celtics. Once again, just like the 1979 NCAA title game, it would be a showdown between Johnson and Larry Bird.

This time, Bird got his revenge as he led the Celtics to the title in seven games. It was one of the most thrilling NBA Finals the league had seen as Bird and Johnson did everything they could to will their teams to victory. Los Angeles won the first game in Boston before losing in overtime in Game 2.

The host Lakers won Game 3 but lost Game 4 in overtime at the Forum. Host Boston won in Game 5. With Johnson leading the way, the Lakers avoided elimination by winning Game 6 in Los Angeles. But back in Boston, the Celtics prevailed 111–102 in Game 7 to win the title. Bird's performance throughout the series earned him the Finals MVP Award. Johnson, meanwhile, had struggled at times and received much of the blame for the Lakers' loss.

"I sat back when it was over and I thought, 'Man, did we just lose one of the great playoff series of all time, or didn't we?'" Johnson said. "This was one of the greatest [postseason series] in history. Yet all you read was how bad I was."[5]

Johnson and the Lakers would get another chance against the Celtics the next season. Los Angeles earned the top seed in the Western Conference with a 62–20 record. The Lakers then breezed through the playoffs' first three rounds and into the NBA Finals. They got their rematch against Boston. This time, the Lakers won, beating the Celtics four games to two. Abdul-Jabbar was selected MVP. For the first time in nine Finals matchups dating to 1959, the Lakers beat the rival Celtics.

The Lakers would be making more championship-round appearances in the future, and Johnson would once again be earning postseason accolades.

Magic Johnson, *right*, embraces Kareem Abdul-Jabbar after the Lakers beat the rival Celtics in six games in the 1985 NBA Finals. Johnson earned his third title.

CHAPTER 5

In May 1987, Magic Johnson received his first NBA regular-season MVP Award. NBA commissioner David Stern is at left, with Lakers owner Jerry Buss at right.

A Magical MVP

During Magic Johnson's first six seasons in the NBA, star teammate Kareem Abdul-Jabbar was the focal point of the Lakers. He was the veteran to whom everyone looked for leadership. Johnson was a star, but Abdul-Jabbar was the leader on offense. During those first six seasons, Abdul-Jabbar never averaged fewer than 21.5 points per game. Johnson had never averaged more than 21.6 during that time, and his career-high average occurred during his second season. Over the next five seasons, Johnson's highest average was 18.8.

But after the Lakers were upset four games to one by the Houston Rockets in the 1986 Western Conference finals, Los Angeles coach Pat Riley knew that the offense's focus had to shift away from Abdul-Jabbar, who was closing in on his fortieth birthday. The focus would switch to Johnson, and he was ready.

Johnson took only two weeks off after the series loss to the Rockets before heading back to the gym. He wanted to be ready to take control of the Lakers when the 1986–87 season started. He later said,

> Somehow, I knew it was going to come down. But I didn't know how it would be communicated, and I didn't know how it would be accepted.
>
> I knew it had to start with me. I had to show everybody I was ready. I had to be an example that I would do whatever it takes to make us a winner.[1]

But in order for Johnson to become "the man" for the Lakers, Abdul-Jabbar had to be fine with that plan. During their time together in Los Angeles, the two superstars got along, but they were never buddies. Their relationship improved after the 1984 NBA Finals defeat to the Boston Celtics. Abdul-Jabbar had called Johnson during the summer, and the two opened up about their lives.

> "He was, in his own way, pushing me to step forward. When you get the eye and the confidence from him, it's like, 'Go for it, man.' He just told me, 'You got to go for it, brother. You got to average over 20 points a game.' When he said that, I said, 'OK.'"[2]
>
> —Magic Johnson, on Lakers teammate Kareem Abdul-Jabbar pushing him to become the team's unquestioned leader

Passing the Torch

It was the beginning of Abdul-Jabbar's passing of the team's leadership to Johnson. Johnson also knew he could improve. His passing was still tremendous and he was an outstanding rebounder, but he knew he could be a better player when shooting the ball. Then he realized what he needed—Abdul-Jabbar's famous hook shot, or the "sky hook" as he referred to it, because Abdul-Jabbar was so tall.

During practice, Johnson and Abdul-Jabbar played the basketball game H-O-R-S-E. Abdul-Jabbar continually shot the sky hook, forcing Johnson to match it. Soon, Johnson's sky hook was nearly as good as Abdul-Jabbar's.

"I watched him so much, I'm saying, 'Hey, that would be a good shot for me,'" Johnson said.

So I started shooting it a lot. I asked him about it, and he said the extension and the release were the key. It doesn't matter if you're taller or nothing, that's a shot I can always get off. I know that, so I go right to it.[3]

Finally an MVP

Thanks to his sky hook, Johnson averaged a career-high 23.9 points in the 1986–87 season and still set his teammates up for easy baskets. He led the NBA with an average of 12.2 assists per game. Los Angeles was never better as a team either. The Lakers nearly set an NBA record for victories in a regular season with a 65–17 record. They fell four games short of tying the then-record 69 victories the 1971–72 Lakers had recorded.

For Johnson, his outstanding play was recognized and he was named the league's regular-season MVP for the first time. His rival-turned-friend Larry Bird had won the previous three MVP Awards, and Johnson wanted one of his own.

"It means a great deal in terms of there's something missing," said Johnson. "That would be like, 'The door's closed now,' so it means a lot.

"I don't want to leave [the NBA] not doing everything. I don't want to leave with Larry having three of them and I don't have any."[4]

Spectacular Playoff Run

The playoffs in the spring of 1987 were nearly as easy for the Lakers as the regular season had been. Los Angeles swept the Denver Nuggets in three games in the opening round and then eliminated the Golden State Warriors in the second round, winning four of the five games. The Lakers followed that by winning all four games they played against the Seattle Supersonics in the Western Conference finals to advance to the NBA Finals.

Once again, the Lakers faced the Boston Celtics. Since Johnson and Bird had entered the league in the 1979–80 season, the Lakers or the Celtics had won all but one of the NBA's titles, with the Philadelphia 76ers taking the crown in 1983. The Lakers had won the championship in 1980, 1982, and 1985, and the Celtics were champions in 1981, 1984, and 1986.

Magic Johnson, *left*, battles Larry Bird for the ball during the 1987 NBA Finals. The Lakers beat the Celtics in six games for their fourth crown of the 1980s.

Johnson helped make sure Boston did not win back-to-back titles as the Lakers downed the Celtics four games to two. The key moment in the series came in Game 4. With Los Angeles holding a two-games-to-one lead, host Boston had a chance to tie the series.

The Celtics took a two-point lead when Bird sank a three-pointer with 12 seconds remaining in the game. After Abdul-Jabbar was fouled, he made only one of two free throws. However, Los Angeles got the ball back after Boston knocked it out of bounds during a battle for the rebound after the second free throw was missed.

Johnson received the ensuing inbounds pass away from the basket. He then drove to the lane and lofted a sky hook over Celtics star big men Kevin McHale and Robert Parish. The shot went into the basket with only two seconds left. The Lakers won 107–106 and grabbed control of the series, leading Bird to comment that you might expect to lose on a sky hook against Los Angeles, but from Abdul-Jabbar, not Johnson.

Repeat?

The Lakers lost in Game 5 at Boston Garden but defeated the visiting Celtics 106–93 in Game 6 to clinch the title. Johnson was chosen as Finals MVP. It was the Lakers' fourth title of the 1980s and the tenth in team history. During the postgame celebration, coach Pat Riley was asked whether the Lakers could repeat as champions the following season. Most coaches back away from that question, saying they are just going to enjoy winning the title right now.

Riley, however, did not evade the question. He always looked for ways to motivate his team. Riley guaranteed that the Lakers would win the NBA title again in 1988.

Riley never backed down from his statement, repeating it throughout the summer and into the start of the 1987–88 season. The motivation seemed to work. The Lakers won their first eight games of the season and then added a 15-game winning streak midway through the season. However, Johnson was not having his best season statistically. He scored three points fewer per game, and his rebounding and assist averages were lower as well.

Riley said his star point guard did not have the same motivation and drive he had during his MVP season. Johnson, however, had also missed ten games because of a strained right groin, and it took him some time to get back into top form when he returned to the lineup.

"I think it's just going back to the same way it was before, to taking me for granted," Johnson said. "'Magic? He's supposed to get a triple-double. He's supposed to have all those assists. He's supposed to be leading the best team in basketball.' Does it bother me? Yes, a little."[5]

Advantage Lakers

The 1987 NBA Finals featured the Lakers against the Celtics for the third time in the 1980s. It was the decade's defining rivalry in the NBA. Boston had defeated the Houston Rockets in the 1986 Finals and was looking for a second straight title. But the Lakers beat the Celtics in six games for the 1987 title. Magic Johnson was named Finals MVP. It was the last of the three times he won the award. At the time, he was the only player to win three MVP Awards in the NBA Finals. He was later joined by Michael Jordan (who went on to earn six) and Shaquille O'Neal and Tim Duncan (who both had three through 2010).

With a healthy Johnson leading the way along with Abdul-Jabbar, forward James Worthy, and shooting guard Byron Scott, the Lakers finished the season with the best record in the NBA once again at 62–20. Unlike in 1987, though, the 1988 postseason road to another title would not be so easy.

Another Title—Barely

In the first round of the playoffs in the spring of 1988, the Lakers swept the San Antonio Spurs three games to none. Things then became more difficult for Los Angeles.

In the second round, the Utah Jazz took a two-games-to-one lead before Los Angeles rallied to win the series in seven games. In the Western Conference finals, the Lakers faced the Dallas Mavericks. The Mavericks had won 53 games during the regular season. The Lakers won the first two games in Los Angeles but then lost two straight in Dallas. The home team won every game in the series. The Lakers won Game 5, lost Game 6, and then prevailed 117–102 in Game 7 to take the series.

In the NBA Finals, the Lakers faced the Detroit Pistons, who were emerging as an NBA power. The Pistons were led by point guard Isiah Thomas, a close friend of Johnson's who was also from the Midwest. Thomas grew up in Chicago, Illinois, and starred at

Indiana University. As in the previous two playoff series for Los Angeles, the series against Detroit took seven games. The Pistons led the series three games to two after winning 104–94 in Game 5 in Detroit. The Lakers headed back to Los Angeles, knowing they needed to win Games 6 and 7 if they were going to repeat.

They did. Los Angeles won 103–102 in a thrilling Game 6 and won its second straight title by edging out Detroit 108–105 in Game 7. Worthy recorded the first triple-double of his career, scoring 36 points, hauling in 16 rebounds, and handing out 10 assists.

Magic's Last Title

The NBA championship that the Lakers captured in 1988 was the last one that Magic Johnson would win during his NBA career. The Lakers qualified for the NBA Finals two more times with Johnson but could not bring home the title. They made a bid for a third consecutive crown in 1989, but the tough and physical Pistons swept them in four games in a rematch. Johnson had to leave in the early portion of Game 3 in that series because of a hamstring injury, and he missed the rest of the series. Going into the matchup against Detroit, Los Angeles had not lost in the 1989 postseason, starting 11–0 with sweeps of Portland, Seattle, and Phoenix.

Under a new coach, Mike Dunleavy, Los Angeles advanced to the 1991 NBA Finals against the Chicago Bulls. The highly anticipated series pitted Johnson against the new NBA king, Michael Jordan, and was exciting. The Bulls won their first title, prevailing four games to one.

Bigger than Bird Versus Johnson?

The Lakers and the Celtics were the teams to beat in the 1980s. But then Michael Jordan entered the league. By the 1990s, the Chicago Bulls and Jordan took over. When the Lakers faced the Bulls in the 1991 NBA Finals, Los Angeles forward Mychal Thompson told reporters, "You can't overhype Magic Johnson versus Michael Jordan. Well, you'll try. But nope, it can't be done."[7]

He was named NBA Finals MVP. For Johnson, the victory was bittersweet but well earned.

"This was the hardest championship season, not just because we went to seven games three times," Johnson said.

Playing against Isiah in a championship is probably the hardest thing I've ever had to do—trying to stay away from each other, trying not to be friends.

That's the most difficult thing I've ever had to go through, staying focused on what I had to do. . . . I know Isiah. His heart is as big as this room.[6]

Magic Johnson defends good friend Isiah Thomas of the Pistons during the 1988 NBA Finals. The Lakers won in seven games. It would be Johnson's last title.

CHAPTER 6

On November 7, 1991, Magic Johnson announces that he is HIV positive and retiring from professional basketball.

A Stunning Announcement

L ate in October 1991, Magic Johnson walked into the office of Dr. Michael Mellman, a team doctor with the Los Angeles Lakers and one of Johnson's personal physicians.

As Johnson walked in, he wondered why Mellman had summoned him. Johnson had been with the Lakers in Salt Lake City preparing for a preseason game against the Utah Jazz. He received a call from Mellman, who told Johnson that he needed to return to Los Angeles. Johnson caught the next plane home and immediately went to Mellman's office.

Johnson assumed Mellman needed to see him because an insurance company rejected Johnson for a life insurance policy. Johnson, however, was not very worried. He felt good. In fact, he was in the best shape of his life. During the off-season, he ran three to four miles (4.83 to 6.44 km) on a treadmill every day and lifted weights for 30 to 45 minutes.

As part of the NBA's effort to increase the popularity of the league oversees, the Lakers had spent part of the preseason in Paris, France, playing in the McDonald's Open. In this tournament, various clubs, mostly from around Europe, competed. The Lakers won the tournament. Johnson was named MVP.

Johnson was feeling healthy. But when he entered Mellman's office, he could tell something was wrong. "He looked straight at me," Johnson said. "'Earvin, I have the test results from your life-insurance physical. It says here that you tested positive [for] HIV.'"[1]

HIV, short for human immunodeficiency virus, is the virus responsible for causing AIDS, or acquired immune deficiency syndrome. AIDS is a disease that destroys the body's ability to protect itself from infection and other diseases. It is transmitted by the exchange of body fluids or blood transfusions. In the case of Johnson, it was because he had engaged in unprotected sex in the past.

Johnson's world was instantly changed. He was told he did not have AIDS. But Johnson, like many people during that era, did not really know the difference between the virus (HIV) and the disease (AIDS). He just knew that one led to the other. Usually, those who tested positive for HIV contracted AIDS within ten years.

Telling His Wife

After hearing the news, Johnson knew he had to tell his wife, Cookie. The two had been together for years but had married just the previous month. Cookie was seven months pregnant with the couple's first child. Johnson was frightened that his wife and future child would be HIV positive.

Cookie was tested immediately, and Johnson was retested to make sure the first results were correct. Two weeks later, the test results came back.

HIV Facts

By the mid-1990s, advances in HIV treatments began to help slow the progression of HIV infection to AIDS. Better treatments also led to a decrease in AIDS-related deaths in the United States.

According to the Centers for Disease Control and Prevention (CDC), at the end of 2006, an estimated 1.1 million people in the United States were living with diagnosed or undiagnosed HIV infection.

African Americans made up only 15 percent of the US population in 2007. Yet, they made up 51 percent of the people diagnosed with HIV/AIDS, followed by whites (29 percent) and Latinos/Hispanics (18 percent). According to the Kaiser Family Foundation, HIV was the leading cause of death for blacks from 25 to 44 years of age.

At the time Johnson tested positive for HIV, many believed HIV was contracted mostly through homosexual sex or intravenous drug use. However, according to a 2007 CDC study, 32 percent of those diagnosed with HIV/AIDS contracted the disease through heterosexual sex. Male-to-male sexual contact accounted for 53 percent of those diagnosed, and 17 percent contracted the disease through drug injection use.

Magic Johnson and his wife, Cookie, leave a church in Lansing, Michigan, after getting married in September 1991.

Johnson again tested positive for HIV. The good news, however, was that Cookie tested negative, meaning that she and the baby were healthy.

While waiting for the test results, Johnson did some research about the HIV virus. He learned that with the proper medical treatment and a proper diet, he could live a normal life for a long time. But his doctors said his normal life could no longer occur on the basketball court. Because of the grueling NBA schedule, they believed that Johnson would weaken his immune system if he played. They felt Johnson should retire—immediately.

It was not easy, but Johnson agreed with them.

My ignorance could cost me my life, but I wanted to try to ensure that no one else would become infected with HIV for the same reason. The following day, I stood at the podium at the Great Western Forum—the place where I had some of my greatest moments as a Laker—and spoke from my heart.[2]

End of a Career

On November 7, 1991, Johnson held a news conference to announce his immediate retirement from the NBA. His announcement was brief. In typical Johnson fashion, it was positive and focused on his future.

I just want to say that I'm going to miss playing. And I will now become a spokesman for the HIV virus because I want people—young people—to realize that they can practice safe sex. And you know sometimes you're a little naive about it and you think it could never happen to you. You only thought it could [happen to] other people, you know, and so on and on, and it has happened, but I'm going to deal with it and my life will go on. And I will be here, enjoying the Laker games, and all the other NBA games around the country. So, life is going to go on for me, and I'm going to be a happy man.[3]

Prepared for the End

Magic Johnson knew his basketball career would eventually end—just not the way it did. He said he had been preparing for the end of his career since he was drafted by the Lakers on June 25, 1979. He did this by studying business opportunities whenever possible.

Johnson knew the effect his announcement would have on his team. Johnson was the focal point of the Lakers, and it would be hard to imagine them taking the floor without their leader. But he did not comprehend the full impact his announcement would have on people outside basketball.

"When I left the Forum, I didn't know that anyone outside Los Angeles had seen the press conference," Johnson said.

I didn't know that it had been broadcast live nationally on CNN and ESPN—and was picked up by many local affiliates of the major networks—until Cookie and I arrived home and the telephone started ringing. My friends were calling from around the country. Some of them said they were going to get tested. Within the next few days I was floored by the media coverage of my infection and by reports that after my announcement thousands of people entered hospitals and clinics all over the nation and asked to be tested for AIDS. Hotlines were unable to answer all of the calls. Condom sales soared, as did donations to AIDS organizations.[4]

Still Healthy

Almost 20 years after his stunning news conference, Johnson still did not have AIDS. According to his doctors, better and more powerful drugs have reduced Johnson's HIV virus to undetectable levels. Thousands of other HIV patients have seen their infections reach undetectable levels thanks to drug treatments.

But that does not mean Johnson and others with HIV are free of the virus. People with undetectable virus levels can still infect others. Johnson has maintained his drug treatment and works out regularly. When Johnson announced he was HIV positive in 1991, he brought a new level of awareness to AIDS. Doctors and AIDS activists hope Johnson's current condition will encourage others to take advantage of the improved treatments and understand the value of maintaining a healthy lifestyle.

"My concern is that people are going to think . . . that he's

Learning about HIV

Seeking some insight into HIV and AIDS, Magic Johnson and his wife, Cookie, visited Elizabeth Glaser. She became infected with HIV in 1981 through a blood transfusion and unknowingly infected her children. Glaser was dying, but she offered some words of comfort to Johnson and asked him to become the "face of the disease."[5] Johnson agreed to her request. To honor his promise to her, he started the Magic Johnson Foundation, which is dedicated to AIDS-related research and outreach. He also agreed to join President George H. W. Bush's National Commission on AIDS.

"Before [Johnson revealed he was HIV positive], people were ostracized, in my estimation, for having the disease. Magic was the person, because his name reached far beyond sports, to make [HIV] acceptable, more a disease than a mark of shame."[8]
—*Basketball commentator Kenny Smith, a former NBA player, in 2006*

cured, that there's a cure for AIDS, therefore, I don't have to worry about being infected," said Lee Klosinski, director of education at AIDS Project in Los Angeles. "I hope people get the message about how important treatment is."[6]

A New Job

With his retirement from basketball in 1991, Johnson understood that he had a new job. That job is to help educate people about HIV and how not to contract the virus.

As he said in 1991,

The way I chose to deal with the HIV infection was to go public. Until last week, I was just like so many other people in this country: I was ignorant of the reality of AIDS. I hadn't paid attention to the statistics that showed that almost one million Americans are HIV-positive, that some 200,000 have AIDS, and that more than 125,000 have died from the disease in the last 10 years. . . . To me, AIDS was someone else's disease. Not for someone like me.[7]

He learned it was for someone like him, and he wanted to change that.

Magic Johnson speaks to reporters in 1991 while announcing he is retiring from the NBA because he is HIV positive. In the years ahead, Johnson would raise awareness of HIV and AIDS.

CHAPTER 7

Magic Johnson talks to students at Walton High School in the Bronx, New York, in March 1992 about the importance of practicing safe sex and staying in school.

A Spokesman and a Dreamer

Taking on the role of AIDS spokesman, Magic Johnson said,

One of the first things I must do, though, is educate myself. My doctors have given me stacks of literature on AIDS, and I intend to read every word before starting my new phase of life. In some ways it'll be another fast break, full-force and all-out. I don't want to undersell my message of safe sex, education and research.[1]

Johnson compared his new role to his life in basketball. Instead of being the point guard for the Lakers, he was now an activist—the point guard for a cause—though still a rookie trying to learn as much as he could about it.

"If anybody thought I could get away with just pretending to be an AIDS activist, then they didn't sit with me . . . listening to people with the disease talk about it," Johnson said. "Everywhere I go, publicly or privately, people tell me that they have HIV or AIDS, or that their brother has it, or their

Magic Johnson meets with President George H. W. Bush in the Oval Office on January 15, 1992, to discuss the need for more federal money to fight HIV and AIDS.

child. This problem is all around us, and it's a very real threat to our country."[2]

True to his word, Johnson has used his celebrity to help raise awareness of HIV and AIDS. In December 1991, he formed the Magic Johnson Foundation, a nonprofit organization designed to help educate as many people as possible about HIV and AIDS.

He has organized exhibition basketball games, fashion shows, and other functions to raise money to fight AIDS. He appeared on television on Nickelodeon, in a program called *A Conversation With Magic*, on March 25, 1992, to answer questions from children about HIV and AIDS. He often visits schools to talk to teenagers. The key, Johnson said, is that he speaks directly to the children and is frank with them about how he contracted HIV and why it was wrong.

Trustees of the Addiction Research and Treatment Corp. (ARTC) and the Urban Resource Institute (URI) gave Johnson the 2004 URI Humanitarian Service

Leaving the Commission

Two months after Magic Johnson announced that he was HIV positive, he attended his first meeting with the National Commission on AIDS. Johnson was hoping that President George H. W. Bush and his administration would help fund research to battle HIV and AIDS.

But he soon learned that the Bush administration was not going to provide as much funding as he had hoped. In an attempt to get more money to fight the AIDS epidemic, Johnson wrote to the president, asking the federal government for $400 million for AIDS research in 1992 and $500 million in 1993. Additionally, Johnson asked for $300 million to be directed to treatment in 1992

and $600 million in 1993. Johnson also wanted a change in the Medicaid policy to fund treatment for people with HIV and not just people with AIDS. Medicaid is the US health program for eligible individuals and families with low incomes and resources.

President Bush wrote Johnson back, thanking him for his letter, but the money never came. Believing his time was going to be wasted, Johnson resigned from the commission in September. In a letter to President Bush, Johnson said he could not serve on a commission whose important work was being ignored and accused the president of dropping the ball concerning the HIV and AIDS crises.

Award at a gala held at the United Nations in New York.

"We've been able to give away probably $5 to $10 million to great HIV and AIDS organizations," Johnson said in 2005 of his foundation.[3]

Fulfilling a Dream

Johnson had a new mission in life, but he could not completely get away from his former life. Johnson loved the sport of basketball and appreciated everything it had given him. Before learning he was HIV positive, Johnson had agreed to be a member of the 1992 Summer Games Dream Team—the first US Olympic basketball team composed of professional players.

Johnson had won championships at the high school, college, and professional levels. But he never had a chance to win a gold medal in the Olympics, and he did not intend to pass up the opportunity.

Magical Moments

On February 9, 1992, three months after his retirement from the Lakers, Magic Johnson jogged onto the floor of the Orlando Arena to a lengthy standing ovation at the forty-second NBA All-Star Game. Although he had not played a single game that season, the fans voted him into the starting lineup for the Western Conference team. He scored 25 points in 29 minutes to lead the Western Conference squad to a 153–113 victory over the Eastern Conference team. Johnson was named the game's MVP. He proved that an HIV-positive person could compete at the highest level.

When it came time for the Dream Team, which also included Larry Bird and Michael Jordan, to assemble and practice, Johnson was healthy enough to participate. After a series of exhibition games and a tournament to qualify for the Olympics, Johnson and his teammates flew to Europe to get ready for the Olympic tournament.

Finally, the Opening Ceremonies for the 1992 Summer Olympics in Barcelona, Spain, took place. Thousands from all around the world participated in the parade of athletes who marched into the stadium. One of those athletes was Johnson, who later said,

> *Marching in the Opening Ceremonies was one of the wildest and most amazing things I've ever experienced. Athletes from other countries started breaking out of line and running over to ask me for autographs, take my picture, or just shake my hand. I'm used to attention, but I couldn't believe that so many athletes from so many different places wanted to meet me.[4]*

It's a Boy

On June 4, 1992, Earvin Johnson III was born to Magic Johnson and his wife, Cookie. Magic and Cookie were proud, and relieved, since both mother and baby tested negative for HIV.

Before the birth of baby Earvin, Johnson had received a call from his son Andre. Andre was born in 1981 to Melissa Mitchell, Johnson's girl-friend at the time. Andre asked what Magic and Cookie were going to name the baby. Magic told him Earvin Johnson III. Andre said that should have been his name. At that time, Andre did not share the same last name as his father. After Magic talked to Cookie, they asked Andre whether he wanted to take John-son's last name. Andre's mother did not mind, and soon there was another Johnson in the family— Andre Johnson.

Let the Games Begin

When the Olympic Games started, the US team, as expected, dominated its opponents. Team USA defeated Angola 116–48 in the opening game and then beat Croatia 103–70. This was followed by victories over Germany (111–68), Brazil (127–83), and Spain (122–81) to close out pool play.

In the quarterfinals, the Dream Team defeated Puerto Rico 115–77. Then came a 127–76 victory over Lithuania in the semifinals. In the final, Croatia gave the United States a tough game at first, but the Americans were able to pull away and win 117–85 to capture the gold medal. Given the talent of its players, the US team was expected to win the medal. But that fact did not make the moment any less magical for Johnson, who commented,

> Although everybody knew we would win the gold medal, it was still a magnificent moment when it finally happened. I almost broke down during the playing of "The Star-Spangled Banner," but I had promised my teammates that I wouldn't cry. Still, it wasn't easy to hold back, and my skin was covered with goose bumps.
>
> Standing on the platform, I said a silent prayer. I thanked God for giving me the strength and the opportunity to come back, to play basketball again, and to be a part of that whole magnificent Olympic experience. It's a memory I will always cherish.[5]

Magic Johnson rejoices during the gold-medal ceremony on August 8, 1992, at the Summer Olympic Games in Barcelona, Spain.

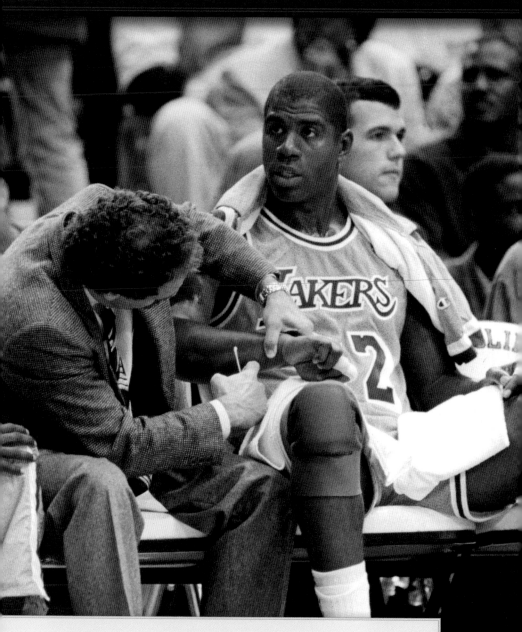

CHAPTER 8

A trainer bandages a cut on Magic Johnson's arm during an exhibition game on November 3, 1992. This was Johnson's last game before he stopped his comeback attempt.

Encore Performance

It was obvious that Magic Johnson still loved to play basketball at the highest level. He proved to everyone that he could still play the game despite his illness. He also decided that he wanted to return for the 1992–93 NBA season and informed the Lakers of his decision. He began working out with Los Angeles and played with the team during the preseason.

"Despite the virus, I was in terrific shape following a year of rigorously working out," Johnson said. "And I couldn't wait for our opening game against the Clippers on November 6. After the Dream Team's great triumph in Barcelona, I had been riding high."[1]

Then, during a preseason game in Chapel Hill, North Carolina, against the Cleveland Cavaliers, Johnson suffered a cut. It was barely visible, but Johnson came out of the game in order to have it bandaged. However, because his arms were perspiring, the bandage would not stick, so trainer Gary Vitti covered it with a sweatband.

Special Diet

When Magic Johnson learned he was HIV positive, one of the first things he had to do was change his diet. He now eats almost no red meat, limited fried food, and lots of chicken, fish, vegetables, and fruit.

Everyone watched, and the mood in the arena seemed to shift. Would the sweatband stay in place? Would Johnson bleed on an opposing player? Though extremely unlikely, the HIV virus could theoretically spread if Johnson's blood came in contact with a cut on another player.

Johnson noticed that everyone seemed scared. Right then, he decided he would not return to the Lakers. "I could see that playing this season wasn't going to be much fun," Johnson said. "And I had always promised myself that if that ever happened, I would leave the game."[2]

The Return—Again

Johnson reluctantly walked away from the game in 1992, ending his five-week comeback on November 2, just before the regular season started. But he could never really let it go. Fear of how the other players would react to playing against him is what forced him to retire. It was not because of a lack of ability or desire.

Utah Jazz forward Karl Malone was one of the most vocal critics of Johnson's attempted return, pointing to his own scars and scabs on his arms as proof of just how physical the game was. "They can't tell me you're not at risk," Malone said of playing against Johnson. "And you can't tell me there's one guy in the NBA who hasn't thought about it."[3]

By 1996, the stigma attached to HIV and AIDS seemed to lessen. Everyone understood the disease a little better. Missing the game he had played since childhood, Johnson announced that he was going to come out of retirement and play for the Lakers once again.

The reception he received from the players was in stark contrast to the one he received in 1992. Johnson said most players understood that if they were to get hit by him, it would not be the end of the world. Utah's Malone said, "I have no problem playing against him, absolutely not. We're more knowledgeable now."[4]

Still, others were fearful of his return, most notably Philadelphia 76ers coach John Lucas. He feared more for the safety of Johnson than the opposing NBA players. "He's killing himself, you know that

Coach Johnson

In 1994, Magic Johnson briefly coached the Los Angeles Lakers after Randy Pfund was let go as coach. Team owner Dr. Jerry Buss asked Johnson if he would coach the team for the final 16 games of the season. Johnson agreed and compiled a 5–11 record as the Lakers finished the season 33–49.

Magic Johnson reacts to the Lakers' play on March 27, 1994.
Johnson served as coach on a fill-in basis to end the season.

don't you?" Lucas asked. "His addiction [to the game] is killing him, and no one is trying to stop him."[5]

Some called for Johnson and any other players with HIV to be banned from playing. Commissioner David Stern, however, was supportive of Johnson. In addition, the NBA had addressed the problem concerning players who were bleeding. All trainers had to wear latex gloves when dealing with open wounds. Bleeding players had to sit on the bench until the bleeding had stopped and the cut had been bandaged.

Back on the Court

Johnson did not listen to Lucas, or any other critic. He returned to the NBA on January 30, 1996, in a game against the visiting Golden State Warriors. This was his first NBA game since June 12, 1991. Playing with more weight than he had during his first stint with the Lakers, Johnson was now a power forward instead of a point guard. But the position switch worked just fine.

Adding to the Family

Magic Johnson and his wife, Cookie, became parents for the second time in 1995 when they adopted a baby girl. Elisa Johnson was born the second week of January in Michigan. The Johnsons picked her up a few days later and took her home to Los Angeles. The Johnsons chose her first name, Elisa.

With 9:39 remaining in the first quarter, Johnson pulled off his warm-ups and entered the game to a loud ovation at the Forum. Johnson was back with the Lakers, and the thrill of watching the team play was back as well. Amazingly, Johnson played as if he had never retired. He dazzled the crowd and players with his passing, including a fake of a no-look pass that allowed Johnson to speed past Latrell Sprewell and down the lane for an easy layup.

The Lakers won 128–118. Johnson finished with 19 points, 10 assists, and eight rebounds, prompting Sprewell to say Johnson was still "the man" after the game. Johnson's teammates were in awe of what they had witnessed on the court.

Lakers guard Eddie Jones said,

It was just amazing. A couple of times, I thought, "How did he see me? How did he throw that pass?" How many guys get to play basketball with a guy they idolized all those years? It's hard to explain what we're all feeling right now.[6]

Johnson went on to play 32 games in 1996, starting in nine. He averaged 14.6 points, 6.9 assists, and 5.7 rebounds per game. After the Lakers lost to the Chicago Bulls in Johnson's second game, Los Angeles won eight straight and compiled a 14–4 record in Johnson's first 18 contests with the team.

Problems Arise

But Johnson was no longer in the prime of his career. He could still score, and he was still an outstanding passer. But Johnson was one step slower on defense, making it easier for an opposing player to get past him. His return also meant reduced playing time for some of the younger players who had been starting or playing a lot of minutes the previous seasons.

The lack of team chemistry haunted the Lakers in the playoffs. Los Angeles faced the Houston Rockets in the opening round. The Lakers had finished with a better record in the regular season, so the first two games of the series were played in Los Angeles.

Houston won the first game 87–83, leading Johnson to complain about playing too much in the low post and not at point guard, which is where he believed he could be more effective. Los Angeles won Game 2, but the Rockets won the next two games to eliminate the Lakers from the playoffs.

Johnson still enjoyed playing basketball, but he no longer had the same level of joy. The game had changed, and so had he. He was no longer the focal point of the

His Own Statue

In February 2004, a 17-foot (5.18-m) bronze statue of Magic Johnson was unveiled in front of fans and former teammates outside the Staples Center in downtown Los Angeles. The Staples Center had been the Lakers' new home arena since 1999.

The giant statue depicts Johnson in his number 32 jersey and dribbling the ball with his right hand while pointing with his left index finger—a familiar image of him when he was directing the Lakers' offense.

During his speech at the statue's unveiling, Johnson said he was amazed and never expected to see a statue of himself.

He also said the statue was a representation of all of his former teammates because they helped him become the player everyone referred to as Magic.

Then, in 2003, twenty-four years after Johnson led Michigan State to its first NCAA basketball championship, the school honored Johnson with a statue outside the Breslin Center—the Spartans' home arena.

The sculpture, which cost $250,000, was named *Always a Champion*. It showed Johnson dribbling the ball with his right hand while directing traffic with his left. At Johnson's request, there was a serious look on his face, not a smile.

Lakers, who wanted to keep Nick Van Exel at point guard. Once again, Johnson made the decision to retire from the NBA, but this time it was on his terms.

"I was satisfied with my return to the NBA, although I would have hoped we could have gone further into the playoffs," Johnson said. "But now I'm ready to give it up. It's time to move on. I'm going out on my terms, something I couldn't say when I aborted a comeback in 1992."[7]

Magic Johnson goes up for a scoop shot on January 30, 1996, against the Warriors. Johnson almost had a triple-double in his first NBA regular-season game in more than four years.

CHAPTER 9

ICAS BEVERAGES

Magic Johnson and his wife, Cookie, pose at "Magic Evolution," an event held in September 2006 in Beverly Hills, California, to celebrate his 25-year business career.

From Superstar to Super Businessman

While growing up, Magic Johnson had learned the value of hard work and how to be smart about money. He watched his parents work hard and save as much money as possible. When Johnson became a member of the Lakers, he became aware that some players who had earned millions of dollars were almost broke when they retired because they had not thought ahead.

Johnson did not want the same fate. He wanted to ensure that he had a career after his basketball days. When he was forced to retire from the NBA in 1991, he was able to handle the sudden change in his career because he had been looking at business opportunities for years and had received good advice from financial advisors.

When Johnson was still playing, he invested in a Pepsi distributorship and a sports memorabilia store. He also founded a T-shirt company. After the Lakers won the NBA title in 1988, Johnson and several of his teammates wore one of his shirts during the celebration. The next day, more than 150,000 of the shirts were sold to fans who had seen them on television.

Johnson was always on the lookout for business opportunities. According to Lon Rosen, Johnson's former agent and a longtime friend,

> *When he would go to a city, he'd say, "I'm not going to sit around and watch soap operas all day. As long as they are flying me around for free, I might as well take advantage of it." So he'd meet with Coke executives when [the Lakers] played the Hawks in Atlanta and Target executives when they played the Timberwolves in Minnesota.*[1]

Johnson eventually worked out a unique joint venture deal with Starbucks chairman Howard Schultz. This enabled Johnson to own some stores, even though stores were generally owned and operated by the main company, not individuals.

Not There for the Photo Opportunity

When Magic Johnson first tried to put together business deals during and after his retirement from the NBA, many of his potential partners turned him down. Johnson said people were more interested in getting an autograph and a picture than making a deal with him.

Schultz said of Johnson,

> *He had a deep sense of compassion and sensibility for the inner city and what he wanted to do. That hit an emotional chord with me. And when the cameras are off and there's no publicity to be had, I've seen him do things that demonstrate a heartfelt commitment to the community.*

Magic Johnson poses with Starbucks chairman Howard Schultz in May 1999 in New York. Johnson and Schultz worked out a deal in which Johnson would own some of the popular chain's coffee shops.

He's willing to make unpaid appearances for us in the inner city at the drop of a hat.[2]

An Urban Focus

Johnson focused his business empire in urban areas. He realized inner-city residents wanted to have access to stores and businesses that residents in the suburbs or more wealthy areas enjoyed. While traveling on team buses during his playing years, Johnson saw the boarded-up businesses of urban areas. He made a promise to himself—when he could, he would return to those areas and do what he could to revive the neighborhoods.

In 1995, Johnson wanted to build a movie theater in a rundown area of Los Angeles that had a lot of gang activity. Johnson took the unusual step of meeting with gang leaders from the Bloods and the Crips. He had a simple request—would the gangs be nice enough to not shoot up the movie theater?

Johnson explained he was helping to build the community. He also said,

> You can't have anything happen at this theater because we're going to hire your cousins, your mothers, your sons and daughters. You come in here and shoot up the place, it might be your own relatives inside.[3]

The theater was taken over by a new owner, Rave Motion Pictures, in 2010. But during its existence as Johnson's theater, it was a centerpiece for the community and was rarely touched by violence. Since that first theater, Magic Johnson Enterprises bought theaters in three other cities, more than 100 Starbucks in 14 states, numerous Burger King restaurants in several states in the Southeast, and several 24 Hour

The entrance to the Magic Theatres is shown in the Crenshaw district of Los Angeles in July 1998.

Fitness/Magic Johnson Sport health clubs. Instead of just lending his names to businesses, Johnson invests in them. He wants to make sure that a business operates to his satisfaction if his name is attached to it.

Not only did Johnson's investments fill a niche market and prove to be successful, they provided job opportunities and beautified the areas. No longer would residents have to see abandoned and decaying buildings. Instead, prosperous businesses began filling

Catering to the Customers

After leading the way to build a 12-screen movie theater in Crenshaw Plaza in Los Angeles, Magic Johnson suggested that since the customers were going to be primarily African American, sweeter drinks should be served as well as spicier hot dogs and buffalo wings. At a Starbucks coffee shop he opened in South Los Angeles, the music was changed to R&B, and sweet potato pie was offered.

the communities in which Johnson was investing.

"His role was quite revolutionary," said Chicago-based real estate investor Quintin Primo. "And you still can't say that urban investment is commonplace today. His involvement still speaks to the vision Magic Johnson has had."[4]

Magic Johnson does not only invest in businesses in urban areas, though; he invests in the people of these communities through his foundation. It is committed to providing opportunities for people living in urban areas. One of its programs, the Community Empowerment Centers, teaches urban youth technological skills and offers educational opportunities. Classes are offered in Web and graphic design, resume writing, and entrepreneurship to name just a few. To date, the centers have helped more than 245,000 disadvantaged youth and provided General Equivalency Diplomas (GEDs) to 1,500 young adults. The foundation also hosts semiannual job fairs, awards grants to nonprofit organizations that serve inner-city communities, and provides college scholarships.

Success Not Easy to Achieve

While Johnson has built a business empire worth an estimated $500 million or more, it has not been easy. Not everything Johnson has tried as a businessman has succeeded. In 1990, he opened a sporting goods store in the Baldwin Hills neighborhood in Los Angeles. He believed that since his name was on the store, it would be a success. What he did not realize, however, was that his merchandise choices were not popular with the young consumers in the area. He had sold only what he liked. Now Johnson makes sure

Magic's Empire

Magic Johnson is involved in many businesses. His business empire includes:

Canyon-Johnson Realty Advisors: Manages the $300 million Canyon-Johnson Fund, which is used to invest capital from pension funds to develop office, residential, and commercial real estate ventures in urban areas.

Johnson Development: Provides services, entertainment, and jobs to underserved communities. It has partnerships with Starbucks Coffee, T.G.I. Friday's, and 24 Hour Fitness Centers.

Magic Johnson Enterprises: Directs and expands partnerships of the Magic Johnson brand, which include deals with Lincoln Mercury, NASCAR, Burger King, and 24 Hour Fitness Center.

Magic Johnson Foundation: Promotes health, education, and social needs for inner-city youth. The foundation has set up college scholarships, HIV/AIDS clinics, and computer centers.

Magic Johnson Theatres: Partners with Loews to build theaters that cater to urban communities.

his business decisions are based with the customer in mind.

As a player, the basketball was often in his hands, allowing him to control his success or not. Everything was up to him. But he has learned that is not always the case in the business world:

> In business, you can do everything right and you still may not get the deal. It was hard to sell retailers and people on the fact that I wanted to invest in urban America. It took me a long time to convince different retailers to come in, so that's why it was hard. And still today, we have a lot going in, but not as many people as we should have investing in urban America. But they're finding out that they have to now in order to grow their bottom line and to grow their business.[5]

The same drive and determination Johnson had during his basketball career has carried over into the business world. Because of his success, former players look at what he has done in order to try to copy it. "He's the envy of every retired player . . . he's built an empire and made such a success of himself off the court, much more off the court than he was on," said former teammate Mychal Thompson.[6]

Sharing His Knowledge

In 2008, Magic Johnson wrote *32 Ways to Be a Champion in Business* and shares what he has learned in the business world.

Future Opportunities

Today, Johnson is more than an entrepreneur and a former basketball player—he has developed a brand that can be felt in 85 cities and 21 states around the country. From catering to staffing services to sport clubs, the Johnson brand is involved in partnerships to stimulate and revitalize underserved communities. In addition to his business ventures, Johnson has three capital management funds that focus on urban investments. He also licenses his image and name and makes personal appearances for companies including Best Buy and Aetna. Each year, Johnson and executives at his company are involved in more than 100 speaking engagements nationally and abroad as well.

Johnson believes in getting personally involved, so customers know he really supports what he is trying to sell or build. Johnson also believes that he can serve as a role model for minorities in the field of business, not just in sports. "What I'm trying to do is leave a legacy for . . . minority people," Johnson said. "I've always considered myself more than just a basketball player."[7]

In October 2010, Johnson surprised the public by selling his minority share in the Lakers. That same month, Johnson sold his 105 Starbucks coffee shops as well. He believed they were good business deals, but he also had a new focus. He wanted to bring the NFL back to Los Angeles. As of 2010, the city had not had a team since the Rams left for St. Louis, Missouri, after the 1994 season. While as of November 2010 nothing had progressed with an NFL deal, Johnson said,

> I haven't had any discussions about the NFL, but I really, really want the NFL to come back to [Los Angeles]. Would I be interested? Of course I will be interested. Have I talked to anybody? No. But I would do that in two seconds.[8]

It is not known where the Magic Johnson empire will expand, but it is sure to grow as Johnson seems to know a good business opportunity when he sees one. As this former basketball great put it, "I'll be looking at every opportunity because I'm a businessman and that's what I do. I look at deals every day."[9]

Magic Johnson speaks to a reporter in 2010. Johnson has expressed interest in helping bring an NFL team back to Los Angeles.

TIMELINE

1959

Earvin Johnson is born on August 14 in Lansing, Michigan.

1974

In his sophomore season at Lansing Everett High School, he plays basketball and is nicknamed Magic.

1977

Earvin leads Lansing High to the Class A title and enters Michigan State University on a basketball scholarship.

1982

The Lakers defeat the 76ers for the NBA crown. Johnson is named Finals MVP.

1985

Johnson and the Lakers win another NBA title, beating Bird and the Boston Celtics.

1987

Johnson is NBA regular-season MVP for the first time and is named Finals MVP.

1979

Johnson leads Michigan State to the NCAA crown, is named Most Outstanding Player, and begins a rivalry with Larry Bird.

1979

Johnson foregoes the remainder of his college career and is drafted by the NBA's Los Angeles Lakers.

1980

Johnson propels the Lakers to the NBA title as a rookie and is named Finals MVP.

1988

Johnson guides the Lakers to their fifth NBA championship of the 1980s.

1990

Johnson is named NBA regular-season MVP for a second consecutive year.

1991

On September 14, Johnson marries Earleatha "Cookie" Kelly.

TIMELINE

1991

On November 7, Johnson announces he has been diagnosed with HIV and will retire from the NBA.

1992

On February 9, Johnson plays in the NBA All-Star Game after fans vote him in. Johnson is the game's MVP.

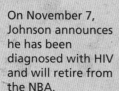

1992

Johnson wins an Olympic gold medal as a member of the US Dream Team.

1994

Johnson coaches the Lakers for 15 games at the end of the season but resigns when the season is over.

1994

In June, Johnson becomes a minority owner of the Lakers.

1996

Johnson returns to play for the Lakers. On January 30, he excels in his first game back.

1992

Johnson resigns
from the National
AIDS Commission.
He cites the
government's
lack of interest in
fighting the disease.

1992

Johnson ends his
comeback try with
the Lakers after
playing in several
preseason games.

1993

Johnson founds
the Johnson
Development
Corporation.

1996

Johnson retires on
his own terms on
May 14.

1997

Johnson founds
Magic Johnson
Entertainment.

2002

Johnson is inducted
into the Naismith
Memorial Basketball
Hall of Fame in
Massachusetts on
September 27.

ESSENTIAL FACTS

DATE OF BIRTH

August 14, 1959

PLACE OF BIRTH

Lansing, Michigan

PARENTS

Earvin Johnson Sr. and Christine

EDUCATION

Lansing Everett High School in Lansing, Michigan

Michigan State University in East Lansing

MARRIAGE

Earleatha "Cookie" Kelly (September 14, 1991)

CHILDREN

Andre, Earvin, Elisa

CAREER HIGHLIGHTS

Johnson won five NBA titles with the Lakers, was named league MVP three times, and was chosen MVP of the NBA Finals three times. In 1992, he won an Olympic gold medal. He was a 12-time NBA All-Star and was inducted into the Naismith Memorial Basketball Hall of Fame in 2002.

SOCIETAL CONTRIBUTIONS

Johnson has been an activist for HIV/AIDS research and prevention. He also started the Magic Johnson Foundation in 1991 as a single-disease organization that worked to raise funds for community-based organizations dealing with HIV/AIDS education and prevention. Johnson's inner-city-focused business investments provided job opportunities and beautified the areas.

CONFLICTS

As part of desegregation in the 1970s, Johnson was bused to Everett High School, which was mostly white, and dealt with teammates who did not want him on the basketball team. Near the end of his career, he tested positive for HIV and fought to teach people about the virus and the stereotypes associated with it.

QUOTE

"What I'm trying to do is leave a legacy for . . . minority people. I've always considered myself more than just a basketball player." —*Magic Johnson*

GLOSSARY

AIDS

Stands for acquired immune deficiency syndrome, a condition, caused by a virus, in which certain white blood cells (lymphocytes) are destroyed, resulting in loss of the body's ability to protect itself against disease. AIDS most often is transmitted by unprotected sexual intercourse, through infected blood and blood products, and through the placenta.

basket

Attached to the backboard, it is suspended 10 feet (3.05 m) from the floor and is 18 inches (45.72 cm) in diameter.

court vision

A player's ability to see everything on the basketball court during play, which helps the player to make better choices when passing the ball.

Dream Team

Name given to the US men's basketball team that won the gold medal at the 1992 Summer Olympics in Barcelona, Spain.

fast break

Beginning with a defensive rebound or a turnover, a player passes the ball to a teammate while that team sprints toward the basket and then quickly shoots before the other team can get back and defend.

Final Four

The name given to the semifinals of the annual NCAA men's and women's basketball tournaments. The Final Four features the West, East, Midwest, and Southeast regional champions.

forwards

The two players on the court who are usually taller than the guards but smaller than the center.

guards

Typically the two shortest players on the team. They usually handle the ball, set up the offense, and pass to teammates for shots.

HIV

Human immunodeficiency virus (HIV) is the agent responsible for causing AIDS. Those with HIV infections ordinarily develop abnormal immune systems and become susceptible to infections and other diseases.

layup

A shot from close range to the basket that usually bounces off the backboard and then into the hoop.

MVP

Initials that stand for Most Valuable Player. The NBA MVP Award is given to the league's player who contributed most to his team during the regular season. An NBA Finals MVP is also honored during the last series of the playoffs.

NBA

Initials that stand for National Basketball Association, which is the major professional basketball league in the United States. It was created in 1949.

NCAA tournament

Yearly competition between 68 teams to determine the men's national championship. Held every March, that month has been nicknamed March Madness.

rebound

When a player grabs a ball that is coming off the rim or backboard after a missed shot.

triple-double

When a player reaches double-digits in three different categories during one game, such as points, assists, rebounds, steals, or blocked shots.

ADDITIONAL RESOURCES

SELECTED BIBLIOGRAPHY

Gottfried, Ted. *Earvin "Magic" Johnson: Champion and Crusader*. New York: Franklin Watts, 2001.

Gutman, Bill. *Magic Johnson: Hero on and off the Court*. Brookfield, CT: Millbrook Sports World, 1992.

Johnson, Earvin, and William Novak. *My Life*. New York: Fawcet Crest, 1993.

FURTHER READINGS

Bird, Larry, and Magic Johnson, with Jackie MacMullan. *When the Game Was Ours*. New York: Mariner Books, 2010.

Johnson, Earvin. *32 Ways to Be a Champion in Business*. New York: Crown Business, 2009.

Pascarelli, Peter. *The Courage of Magic Johnson: From Boyhood Dreams to Superstar to His Toughest Challenge*. New York: Bantam Books, 1991.

WEB LINKS

To learn more about Magic Johnson, visit ABDO Publishing Company online at **www.abdopublishing.com**. Web sites about Johnson are featured on our Book Links page. These links are routinely monitored and updated to provide the most current information available.